Ever since humans have been on Earth, they have raised their eyes to the sky and been astonished by its mysterious beauty.

EARTH, SKY, AND BEYOND

A Journey Through Space

by Jean-Pierre Verdet

illustrated by Pierre Bon

translated by Carol Volk

LODESTAR BOOKS

Dutton   New York

Copyright © 1993 by l'école des loisirs, Paris

English translation copyright © 1995 by Penguin Books USA Inc.

All rights reserved.   CIP Data available.

Translated by Carol Volk

First published in the United States in 1995 by Lodestar Books,

an affiliate of Dutton Children's Books,

a division of Penguin Books USA Inc.,

375 Hudson Street, New York, New York 10014

Published simultaneously in Canada by McClelland & Stewart, Toronto

Originally published in France in 1993 by l'école des loisirs

Printed in Hong Kong   ISBN: 0-525-67513-2

First Edition   10 9 8 7 6 5 4 3 2 1

Migrating birds, such as ducks or wild geese, travel in tight formation, sometimes 3 or 4 kilometers up in the sky.

Eyeing their targets, birds of prey slowly glide and circle a few dozen meters above the ground.

Poplar trees are about thirty meters tall, but eucalyptus and sequoia trees grow to more than 100 meters.

Butterflies flutter just above the flowers and shrubs.

The sky doesn't begin where the stars shine
or even where the clouds float.
The sky touches the tips of the trees
and even the blades of grass at our feet.

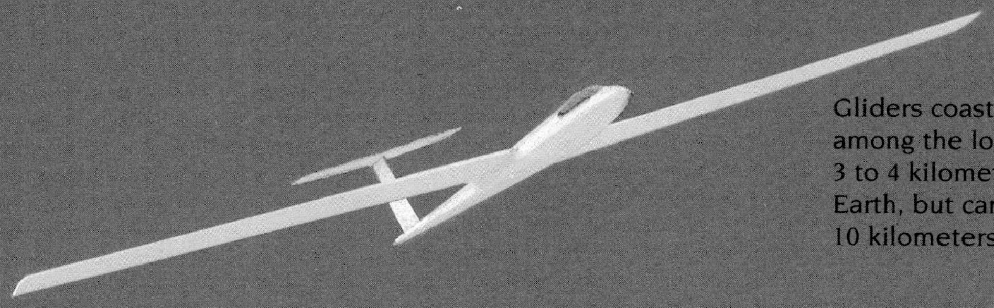

Gliders coast through the air
among the lowest clouds,
3 to 4 kilometers above
Earth, but can go as high as
10 kilometers.

These big storm clouds, called cumulonimbus, develop an anvil shape that can extend up to 8 kilometers high.

Jet planes fly above the clouds at an average altitude of 10 kilometers. The weather is always pleasant for their passengers.

The sky is bright and blue because the light of the Sun reflects off gas particles in the atmosphere. The higher one goes, the less atmosphere there is, and the darker the sky becomes.

Spy planes fly near weather balloons. They survey every corner of Earth.

Earth is surrounded by a mixture of gases called the atmosphere. It is the air we breathe. Winds develop in the atmosphere, and clouds that bring rain, snow, or hail also form there.

Large weather balloons study the atmosphere to predict the weather. They rise to a height of 45 kilometers.

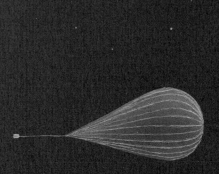

The space shuttle takes off from the ground like a rocket and returns to Earth like a glider. It is capable of transporting satellites 200 to 400 kilometers into space and can go back to repair them.

Now we are above the atmosphere,
where air no longer exists.
We couldn't live here.
The stars shine in a completely black sky.

The satellite Spot roves
850 kilometers above Earth.
It observes forests, farms,
and lakes. In 1986, Spot
took pictures of New York,
in which every street,
monument, and garden is
visible.

Seen from Meteosat, Earth is a big white-and blue ball—a sphere of rock and water surrounded by clouds. The oceans and seas occupy more surface than the land.

At an altitude of 36 000 kilometers, the European satellite Meteosat always sits above the same point on Earth. It observes large masses of clouds and sends images to meteorological stations on the ground.

Up to the stars
that brighten our lives;
Out to the Moon,
which lights up our nights;
On to the Sun,
dazzling star of our days.

The Moon is our satellite.
Only 385 000 kilometers away
from Earth, it revolves around
us in a little more than 27 days
and accompanies us in our
annual revolution around
the Sun.

In July 1969, three
Americans realized one of
humankind's oldest dreams:
to land on the Moon.
After four days of
traveling through space,
Neil Armstrong became the
first man to set foot on
Earth's only satellite.

The spacecraft Apollo headed
toward the Moon. It was
composed of two parts:
One deposited the astronauts
on the lunar surface, and the
other circled the Moon while
waiting for them.

The Moon is covered with
vast dark areas that we
call seas and with vast light
areas that we call continents.
In reality, there are no seas
on the Moon, only great
plains covered with a gray
dust. The light areas are hills
and mountains.

Fixed in place above the lunar horizon, Earth is highly illuminated. Seen from the Moon, Earth appears three times as bright as the Moon does when seen from Earth. This is because Earth's clouds reflect light from the Sun so well.

The lunar jeep is the most expensive car in the world. In 1972, it enabled the American astronauts to visit Mount Descartes; they took short trips, traveling about a dozen kilometers at a speed of 15 kilometers per hour.

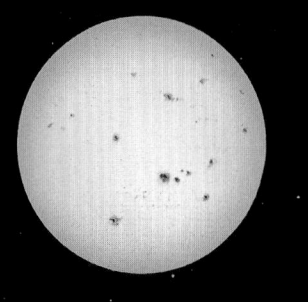

The Sun lights up Earth and the Moon. The Sun is so luminous because it is a very hot ball of gas 1 400 000 kilometers in diameter. The surface temperature is 6 000 degrees Celsius (C), but at its center, the temperature reaches 15 million degrees.

The Moon doesn't shine with its own light but reflects light coming from the Sun. The Moon has no atmosphere, no wind or rain, so its surface can't wear down. The tracks left in the lunar dust by the astronauts will testify to their passage hundreds of thousands of years from now.

We've already traveled 150 million kilometers!
The Sun is near. We can see the bubbling of
its surface and a large arch of burning matter
that shoots into the sky and falls back. The
Sun has been burning for some 5 billion years.
It is in mid-life; astronomers believe that in
another 5 billion years, it will shrink and cool.

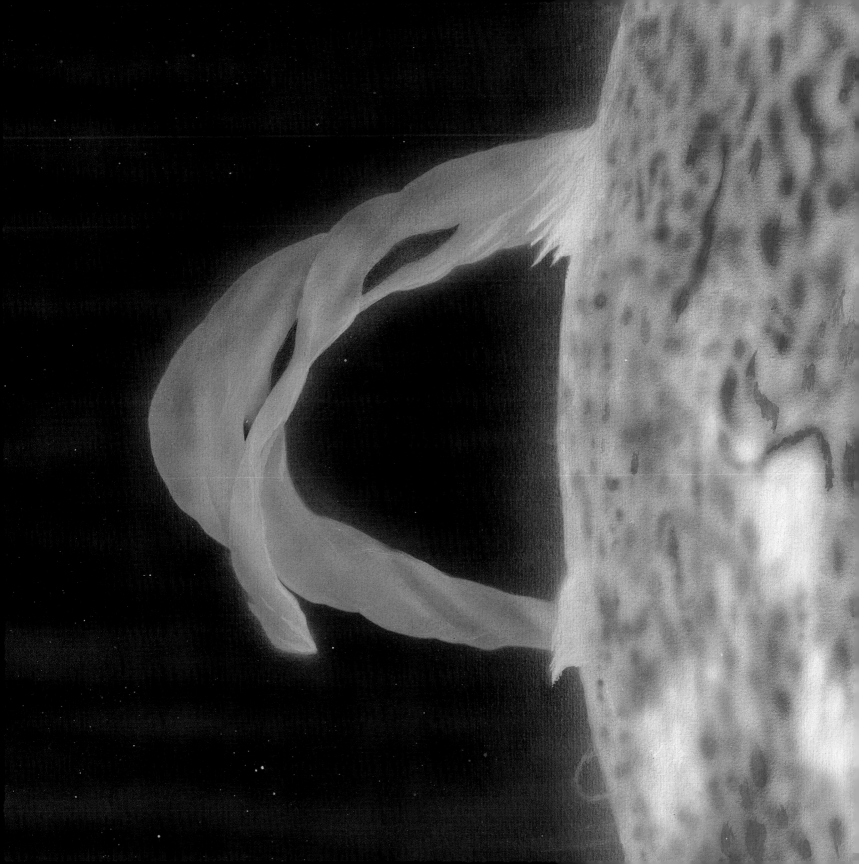

The Sun burns in a black sky.
Some spots on the Sun's surface
are really places that appear
dark because they are not
quite as hot as the areas
surrounding them.

This bright little ball with a
long tail of gas is a comet. It
comes from very far away,
approaches the Sun, and
departs again, only to return
hundreds or thousands of
years later.

Far from Earth, we are weightless; we float in space,
and there is no up or down. A greater journey
now awaits us: We are going to head farther out
into space. First we'll visit the solar system—an
ensemble of planets, satellites, comets, and
meteorites, all revolving around the Sun as if they
were attached to it.

The first planet we encounter
is Mercury, a little world that
has been burned by the nearby
Sun. Mercury's diameter is
barely 4 900 kilometers—about
three times smaller than the
diameter of Earth.

Venus is the planet that most
resembles Earth. It is the same size
but has a heavier atmosphere, which
retains the Sun's energy so well that
the temperature is stifling—over
400° C. Venus revolves around
the Sun in 225 days.

Mercury, Venus, and Mars are called terrestrial
planets because they resemble Earth. Small
in size, with a hard surface on which one can
walk, they have either a light atmosphere or no
atmosphere at all. Few satellites, if any, revolve
around these planets.

As we've been traveling toward the Sun,
Earth has moved. Once more we meet our
planet with its faithful and sole satellite,
the Moon. Together they will make the
940-million-kilometer journey around
the Sun.

The Viking spacecraft, which landed on Mars in 1976, caused disappointment in many dreamers: Mars is a lifeless desert of sand and rock. Martians don't exist.

Mars has two battered-looking little planets, Phobos and Deimos. Here we see Phobos. Deimos must be hidden behind the planet.

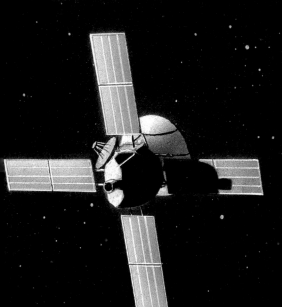

Mars is called the red planet because its surface rocks contain iron that has rusted and given them color. This bloodlike color is the reason the planet is named after Mars, the Roman god of war. Humans have long believed that Mars was inhabited and even thought they could see canals built by Martians.

Beyond Mars, we pass through a large
ring of stones, rocks, and tiny planets, or
asteroids, that are only a few kilometers
in diameter. Astronomers think that this
matter is from a planet that exploded or
never managed to take form.

Here is Jupiter, the king of the planets.
Its diameter is eleven times that of Earth.
More than a thousand Earths could be
hidden inside it. Large bands of colored
clouds appear on its surface; the big
orange eye we see toward the bottom,
called the Great Red Spot, is a cyclone as
big as Earth.

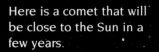

Here is a comet that will
be close to the Sun in a
few years.

Jupiter has sixteen satellites,
four of which are fairly large.
Of these four main satellites,
Io is the one closest to its
planet. It has many active
volcanoes.

Next comes Europa,
which is as big as our
Moon. Its surface is
covered with many
cracks that extend
over thousands of
kilometers.

We are now entering the domain of
the large planets. Unlike terrestrial
planets, these balls of cold gases
have no hard surface on which to walk.
Their very heavy atmospheres are
composed of unbreathable gases.

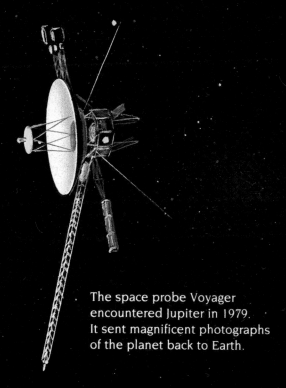

The space probe Voyager
encountered Jupiter in 1979.
It sent magnificent photographs
of the planet back to Earth.

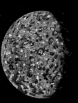

Ganymede is Jupiter's largest
satellite. Its surface, like that of
the Moon, is riddled with
craters.

Most of the large planets
are surrounded by a ring of
ice-covered dust and rocks,
but Saturn's ring is the
prettiest. You can admire it
with a small telescope.

Saturn has nineteen satellites, some of
which are tiny. The first one we see as we
move away from Saturn is Mimas. The
space probe Voyager detected a crater
on Mimas 130 kilometers in diameter
and 10 kilometers deep.

Next come Enceladus and Tethys.
Tethys, which we see here, is three
times the size of Mimas; it measures
1000 kilometers in diameter and
revolves at a distance of 300 000
kilometers from Saturn.

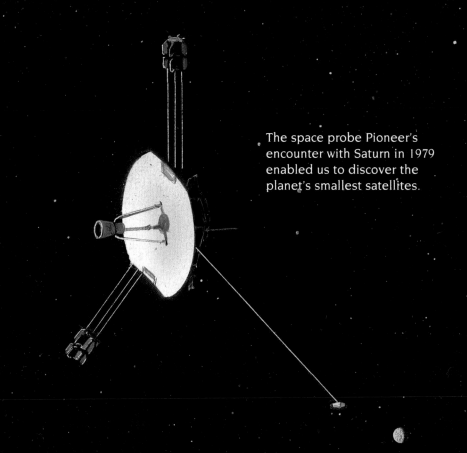

The space probe Pioneer's
encounter with Saturn in 1979
enabled us to discover the
planet's smallest satellites.

Phoebe is the farthest of
Saturn's satellites, revolving
more than 12 million
kilometers away from its
mother planet.

Approximately the same size
as Mercury, Titan is the largest
of Saturn's companions. Its
diameter is one and a half times
that of the Moon. Titan is
surrounded by an atmosphere of
orange-colored haze.

In 1781, Sir William Herschel, an English astronomer of German origin, was the first person to see Uranus, which looks very similar to Saturn.

Before the telescope was invented, in about 1610, people observed the sky with their naked eyes. All they could see were thousands of stars and five planets: Mercury, Venus, Mars, Jupiter, and Saturn.

But with the invention of the telescope, a new world suddenly appeared: millions and millions of stars, planets that were previously invisible, and fine clouds of gas.

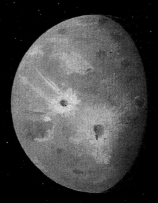

Uranus has fifteen satellites. Pictured here are Titania, the largest of these satellites, and Umbriel, the most mysterious. Umbriel is covered with craters and gray dust. Both satellites are composed of a mixture of rock and ice.

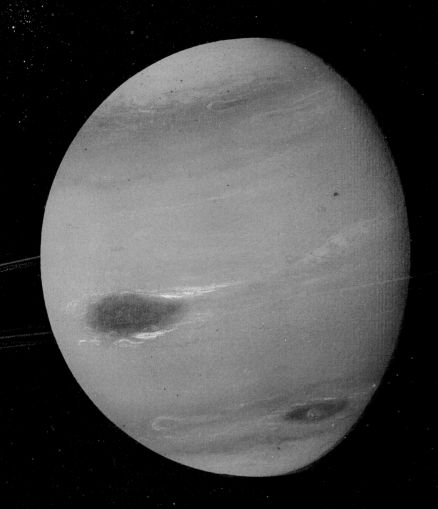

Neptune was discovered in 1846,
thanks to a famous astronomer,
Urbain Le Verrier. His calculations
revealed the position of this planet
in the sky even before it was seen
through a telescope.

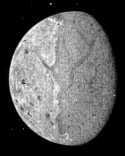

Triton, the most beautiful of
Neptune's eight satellites, has
a surface covered with ridges,
fissures, craters, and plains.

Pluto, the most distant of the
known planets, was discovered in
1930. Pluto is very small compared
to the large planets; perhaps it is a
former satellite that escaped from
Neptune's attraction.

But Pluto has its own companion,
named Charon. Three times smaller
than the Moon, it revolves 20 000
kilometers away from Pluto. It is so
small and so far away that we know
almost nothing about it.

We are now reaching the outer
limits of the solar system. The Sun,
6 billion kilometers away, looks like
nothing more than a bright dot. It's a
cold world here: The temperature on
Pluto is –210° C.

Here, the space probe Voyager has just
left the solar system and faces a great
void. It will have to travel billions of
kilometers before reaching a star. In its
path, it will encounter only a few atoms
of gas and a few specks of dust.

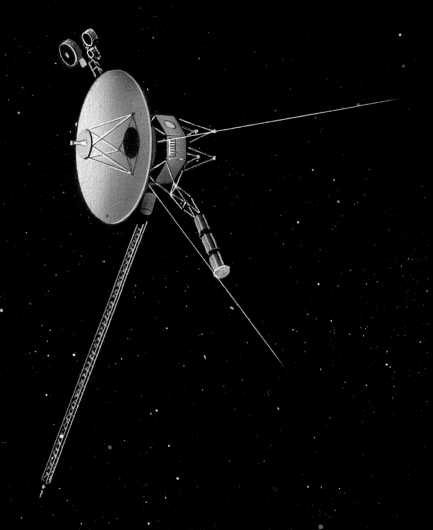

Small, glittering lights appear wherever
we look. They are stars separated by
billions of kilometers. Stars like the Sun:
some smaller, some larger, some younger,
some older. Yellow ones, like the Sun, but
also blue ones, which are hotter, and red
ones, which are colder. A world of suns,
both similar to and different from one
another . . . like people.

Another sun, lost in the universe. Perhaps it is surrounded by planets, perhaps not. Maybe one of these planets has life on it; maybe not. There are so many stars in the world.

The Horsehead Nebula: This dark nebula stands out against a bright cloud and owes its name to its distinctive shape.

The Lyra Nebula is the
luminous remains of a star
that exploded long ago.

The universe has more than just stars.
There are also great clouds of gas and dust.
Some clouds are dark and hide a piece of
the universe from us, but others are bright
and colorful.

Our Sun belongs to
a large family of billions
of stars: our galaxy.
In certain places, the
stars are so close
together they give the
appearance of a long
ribbon of white light.
That's why our galaxy is
called the Milky Way.

Our galaxy is a tremendous vortex that turns slowly around its center. A complete rotation takes 250 million years. Billions of stars swarm in its center, while long branches of stars and gases develop in spirals around them.

Many other galaxies exist in
the universe. Stars group
together in flattened or
spherical galaxies. Billions
and billions of kilometers
separate these large families.
But galaxies can also form
groups, and the vast sky
is filled with clusters of
families of millions or
billions of stars.

How far does the universe go?
What is the shape of the universe?
How are the galaxies arranged?
These are all enigmas that astronomers
are trying to decipher.

Index